FOR OLDER CHILDREN

Featuring 19 songs by Kathie Hill, Chris Marion, David Hampton, Dennis Kurtilla, Twila Paris, Buryl Red, Bill George, JoAnne and Milton LeDoux, Don Schlosser, Carter Robertson, Cathy Spurr, Debbie McNeil, Angela Kelly, and Anita Wagoner

Songs and Hymns Arranged by: Don Schlosser, Barny Robertson, and Randy Smith

Tracks Sequenced by Barny Robertson

Music Engraving by Allen Tuten, Compute-A-Chart

Video by Star Productions

Cover Design by Maksimowicz Design

Design Coordinator, Karla Graul

Illustrations by Bron Smith

Need to order additional MADE FOR PRAISE Volume II materials?

See following page for product listing and ordering information.

0-7673-0831-X

CONTENTS

★ *Titles in italics indicate color teaching pages.*

See *Made for Praise for Older Children, Volume 2 Leader's Guide* (ISBN 0-7673-0831-X) for all piano accompaniments not found in this book.

Whatever Is True

*Melody is in the lower voice.

26
guards our hearts and fills our minds
Bb2
C/F
F
Csus/Bb
Csus
C
29
with His peace that leaves fear be - hind.
And when our
Dm
C
Bb2
F2/A
F/C
F2/C
C
C7/Bb
33
(opt. div.)
anx - ious thoughts be gin to cloud our way,
He re -
F/A
Gm
Dm7
F/C
Bb2
F/A
37
minds us to stand up strong and say:
Gm
F/A
Gm/A
F/Bb
C/Bb
Csus

40
What-ev-er is true, what-ev-er is hon - or-a - ble,
C C7sus
Bb
Csus C
43
(opt. div.)
unis.
think a - bout these things. What-ev - er is right, what-ev - er is
Bb
F
Bb
46
(opt. div.)
unis.
pure and love - ly,
If there's an - y-thing
C
C/D Dm
F/C
49
(opt. div.)
ex - cel - lent a - bout it, If it's worth giv-ing praise,
Bb
C
A

52
unis.
Then let your mind be filled with the pow - er of these
Dm
Bb
C/Bb
Gm9
Bb
C
55
things.
1
What-ev-er is true,
2
Then let your
Bb2
F
Bb/C
F
58
mind be filled with the pow - er of these things.
Bb
C/Bb
Gm9
Bb
C
Bb2
61
(opt. div.)
The pow - er of these things!
Fsus
Gm9
Gm7/D
Bb
Bb/C
C/Bb
F

We Need a Shepherd Medley

Arranged by Barny Robertson

*"We Need a Shepherd," Words and music by CATHY SPURR and DEBBIE McNEIL.

**Melody is in the lower voice.*
For accompaniment see Leader's Guide, p. 103.

(opt. div.)
We need a Shep-herd for this day and age.
We need a Shep-herd to show us the way,
Keep - in' our hearts from go - in' a - stray.
We need a Shep-herd for this day and age.
unis.
Oh, we need a Shep - herd,
Oh, we need a
Shep - herd.
Oh,
we need a Shep - herd.

*"Savior, Like a Shepherd Lead Us," Words by DOROTHY THRUPP. Music by WILLIAM BRADBURY.

*"He Leadeth Me! O Blessed Thought," Words by JOSEPH H. GILMORE. Music by WILLIAM B. BRADBURY.

What an Awesome Power

Words and Music by
DON SCHLOSSER

8
love best love a heart could find. What an awe-some
Em7 D/F♯ C/G G2/A G/A
10
ho - li-ness What an awe-some friend; What an awe-some
D F♯m/C♯ Bm D/A
12
grace, like a warm em-brace that-'ll nev - er end.
Em7 Cmaj9 Em/D D F/D Em/D
14
1 2
What an awe-some
1 Em/D D 2 Em/D D

16
GROUP 1 (rap)
Awe-some pow - er is in His arm; He can res - cue His child from harm.
D
Dm
Em
D
D
18
With His pow - er He fights for me; He has nailed down the vic - to - ry!
D
Dm
Em
D
D
20
GROUP 2 (rap)
Like a gal - ax - y, His awe-some grace a - maz - es me;
D
Dm7
Em
D
D
22
It's still a mys-ter-y how God can care so much for me
D
Dm7
Em
D
D

24
GROUP 3 (rap)
Ho - li-ness, He dwells in ho - li-ness; He reigns in
D
Dm7
Em
D
D
26
pur - i - ty, and He is chang - ing me to know His
D
Dm7
Em
D
D
28
GROUP 1
Awe-some pow - er is in His arm; He can res - cue His child from harm.
GROUP 2
Like a gal-ax-y, His awe-some grace a - maz - es me;
GROUP 3
Ho - li-ness, He dwells in ho - li-ness; He reigns in
D
Dm
Em
D
D

30
With His pow - er He fights for me; He has nailed down the vic - to - ry!
It's still a mys - ter - y how God can care so much for me!
pur - i - ty, and He is chang - ing me; that's right!
D
Dm7
Em
D
D
Fm7
32
CHOIR
What an awe - some pow - er;
What an awe - some
Ebm7
Ab
Ab2
Bb
Eb
Gm
D
34
mind;
What an awe - some love,
best love a heart could
Cm
Eb
Bb
Fm7
Eb
G

36
find
What an awe-some ho-li-ness;
What an awe-some
Db/Ab
Ab2/Bb
Ab/Bb
Eb
Gm/D
38
Friend;
What an awe-some grace, like a warm em-brace that-'ll nev-er
Cm
Eb/Bb
Fm7
Eb/G
40
end.
What an awe-some grace, like a warm em-brace
Fm/Eb
Eb
Fm7
Dbmaj9
43
That-'ll nev-er end
Dbmaj9
Eb
Gb/Eb
Fm/Eb
Fm/Eb
Eb

All That I Need

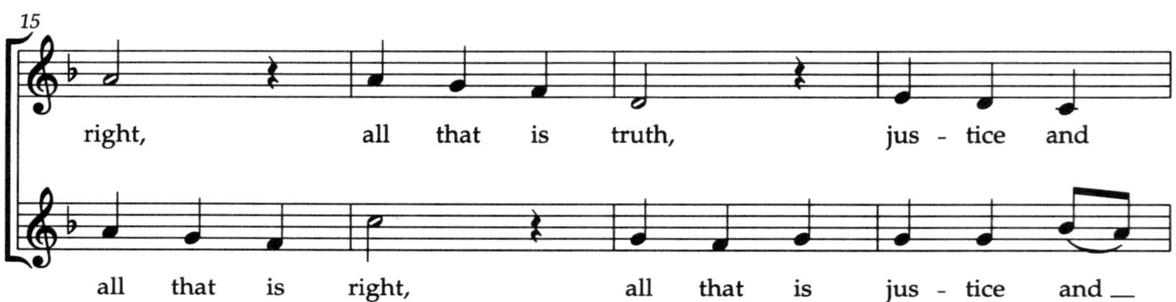

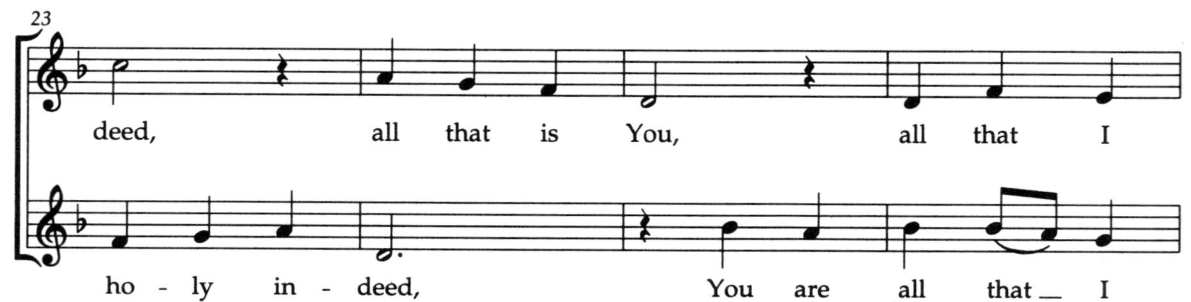

For accompaniment see Leader's Guide, p. 109.

27
1
2
need.
2
1
2
need.
33
2
mf
All that is good, all that is
2
mf
All that is good,
38
right, all that is truth, jus - tice and
all that is right, all that is jus - tice and
42
light; All that is pure, ho - ly in -
light; All that is pure,
46
deed, all that is You, all that I
ho - ly in - deed, You are all that I

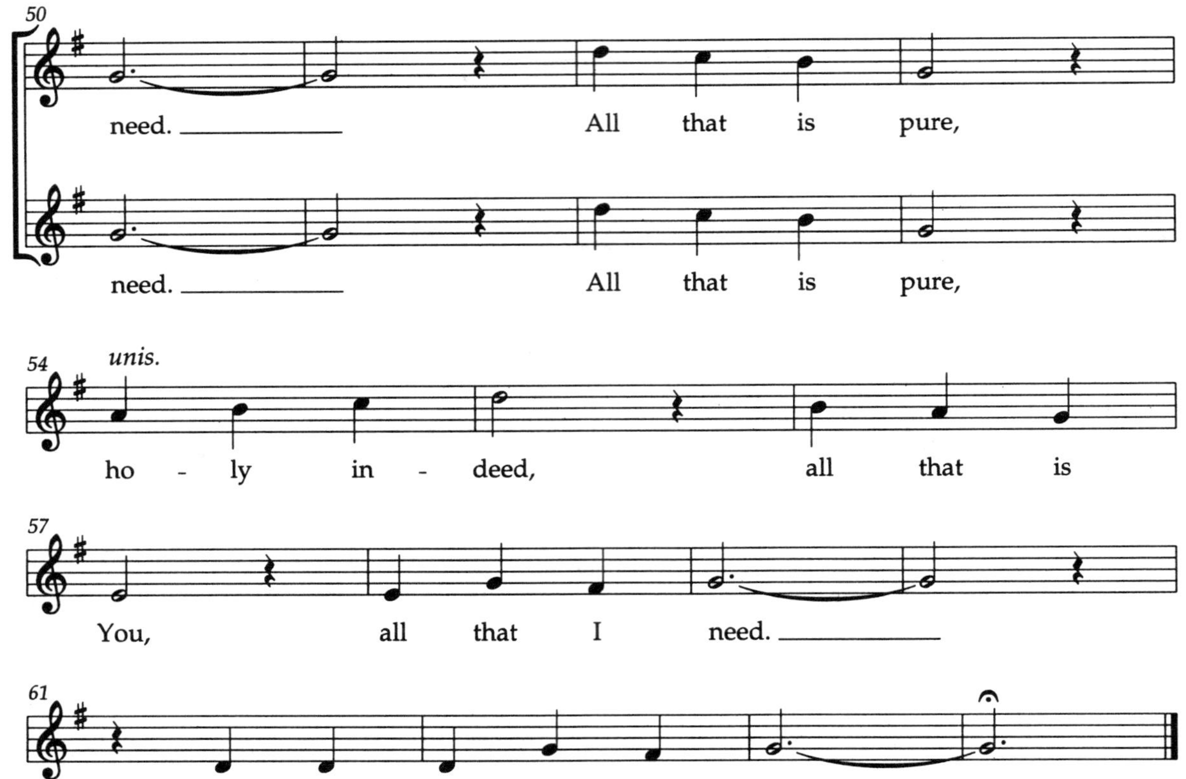
50
need. ___ All that is pure,
need. ___ All that is pure,
54
unis.
ho - ly in - deed, all that is
57
You, all that I need. ___
61
You are all that I need. ___

I Need a Good Friend

Words and Music by
ANITA WAGONER
Arranged by Randy Smith

11
I need a good friend to en - cour - age me.
D
Bm7
E7(♭9)
A7
D
13
I need a wise friend to be my guide,
D
Bm7
Em7
A7
15
who, when I'm lone - ly, will be by my side;
D
Bm7
E7(♭9)
A7
3
17
And when I choose the wrong way to go,
D
A
D
G

19
I need a good friend who will tell me so. I need you, _
D Bm7 E7(♭9) A7 D G
21
_ you need me; _ It's called loy - al - ty, _ lift - ing
(G) G♯dim D/A
23
up _ one an - oth - er. You need me, _
A Bm7 A7/C♯ D Em D/F♯ G
25
_ I need you; _ so let's see what we can do to
(G) G♯dim D/A
3
3

27
let the world know that Christians love each other
E F♯m7 E7/G♯
G/A
29
GROUP 1 f
I know my Savior,
GROUP 2 f
I know my Savior will
A♭/B♭
E♭ Cm7
f
31
His words of wisdom,
walk with me;
His words of wisdom will
Fm7 B♭7
E♭ Cm7

33
But when the world a - round is
help me see.
But when the world a - round is
F7(♭9)
B♭7
E♭
B♭
3
35
CHOIR
crum - bl - ing,
I need a good friend to en -
E♭
A♭
E♭
Cm7
37
cour - age me.
But when the world a - round is
F7(♭9)
B♭7
E♭
E♭
B♭

39
crum - bl - ing, __
I need a good friend to en -
Eb
Ab
Eb
Cm7
41
cour - age me. __
I need you __ to ac - com -
F7(b9)
Bb7
Eb
Ebdim
43
pa - ny me. __
I need a good friend to en -
Ebdim
Eb/Bb
Cm7
3
45
(opt. div.)
cour - age me. __
F9
Bb7
Eb
Eb/G
Ab
Ab/Bb
Eb

Jesus Is All the World to Me

20
Both times - CHOIR
I would fall;
I am His own.
When I am sad, to
He sends the sun - shine
A9 Am D7(♭9) Gmaj7 Am7 D6
25
Him I go,
and the rain,
No oth - er one can cheer me
He sends the har - vest's gold - en
Bm7 B♭7(♭5) Am7 D7 Bm7 E7 Am7
30
so;
grain;
When I am sad,
Sun - shine and rain,
He makes me
Har - vest of
D7 Em E♭aug G/D
34
glad; He's my
grain; He's my
1
friend.
Bm7 E7(♯9) Am7 D7(♭9) Gmaj7 Cmaj7

39
2
friend.
B
C#m7
B/D#
Em
Am7
D7(b9)
Gmaj7
44
3. Je - sus is
f
Cmaj7
Em/B
Bbm7
Eb7(b9)
Ab
48
all the world to me, and true to Him I'll be;
Gm7(b5)
C7/E
Fm
Fm/Eb
Db2
Eb7/Db
Cm7
54
Oh, how could I this friend de - ny, When
F7(b9)
Bbm7
Eb7
Eb7/Db
Cm7
F7(b9)

59
He's so true to me?
Fol - low - ing
Bb13 Ab/Bb Bb/D Eb7 Eb7(b9) Abmaj7
64
Him I know I'm right,
He watch-es o'er me day and
Db/Ab Eb/Ab Db2/Ab Abmaj7 Bbm7 Cm7 Bdim
70
night;
Fol - low - ing Him by day and
Eb7/Bb Fm7 Gb13 Ab
3
74
night, He's my friend.
F7(b9) Bbm7 Eb9 Ab Abmaj7

78
Je - sus is
Db
Dbmaj7
Bbm7
Eb7(b9)
Ab
82
all
the
world
to
me;
He's
Db
Dbmaj7
C
Csus
D
C7
E
Fm
Bbm7
86
my
friend.
Je - sus
Eb7(b9)
Ab
Dbmaj7
Bbm7
90
is
my
friend.
Eb13
Dbmaj7
Absus
C
Ab
C
Bbm7(b5)
Dbm
Eb
Ab2(no 3)
Ab6,9

Friendship Rap

Words and Music by
ANITA WAGONER
Arranged by Barny Robertson

07 *Funky rap* (♩ = 144) 8

CHOIR *(rap)* *mf*

Friend - ship, you know I'm talk - in' 'bout

11 friend - ship, the kind of friends you want to hang with.

14 If I could on - ly have one gift, I think I'd ask for a

17 friend - ship, friend - ship with you.

20 2

I want to find a friend who will en -

24 cour - age me, you know; I want to find a friend who al - ways

26 helps me see that if I on - ly fol - low Je - sus, I will

28 al - ways be the kind of friend who al - ways lives with oth - ers

30 peace - ful - ly, like you! 9

For accompaniment see Leader's Guide, p. 113.

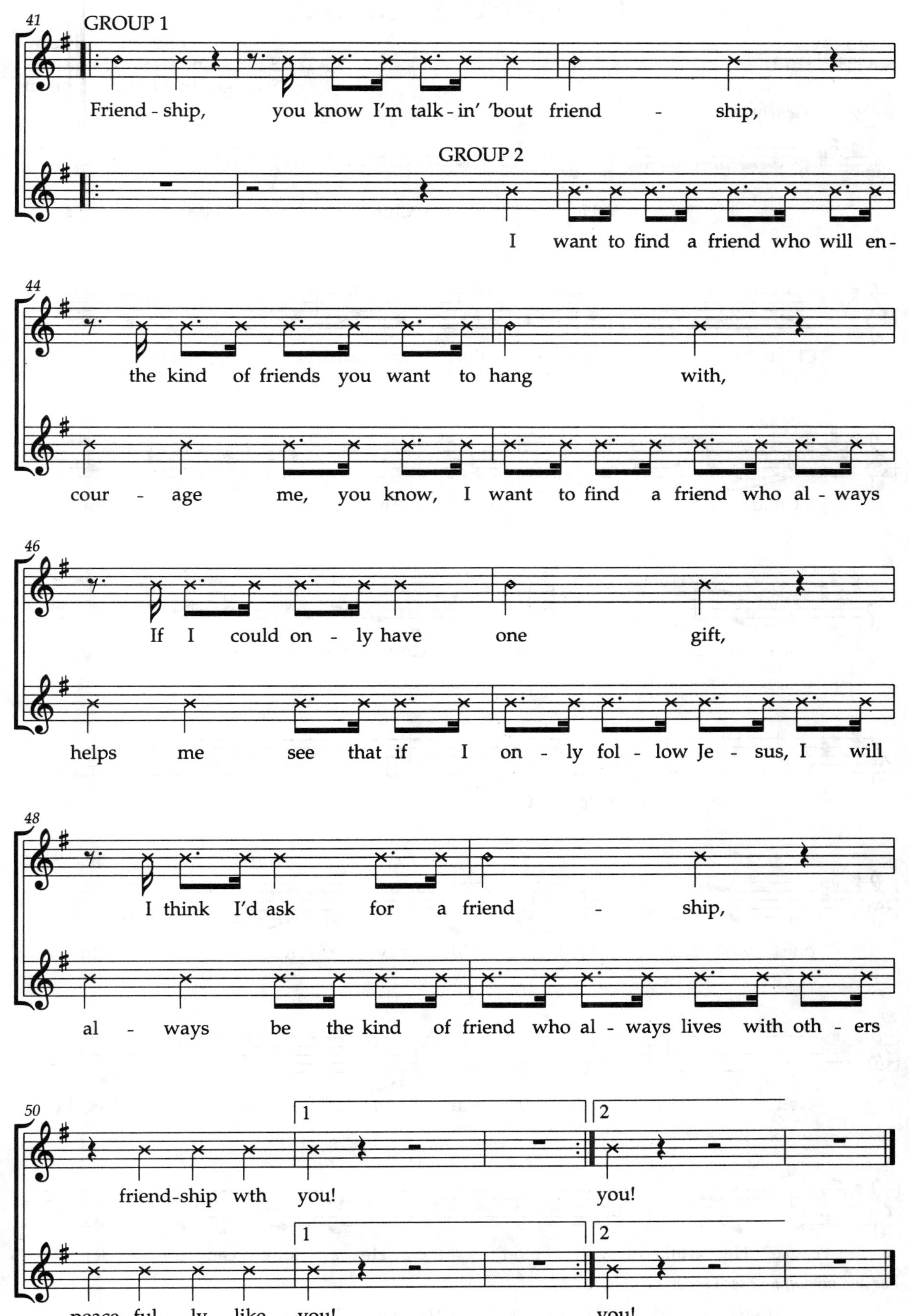
41
GROUP 1
Friend - ship, you know I'm talk - in' 'bout friend - ship,
GROUP 2
I want to find a friend who will en -
44
the kind of friends you want to hang with,
cour - age me, you know, I want to find a friend who al - ways
46
If I could on - ly have one gift,
helps me see that if I on - ly fol - low Je - sus, I will
48
I think I'd ask for a friend - ship,
al - ways be the kind of friend who al - ways lives with oth - ers
50
1
2
friend-ship wth you! you!
peace - ful - ly, like you! you!

Heaven's Child

Words by
KATHIE HILL

Words and Music by
KATHIE HILL and CHRIS MARION
Arranged by Barny Robertson

For accompaniment see Leader's Guide, p. 118.

36
stand how we need. Him as our friend.
40
CHOIR
Heav - en's Child, Heav - en's
44
Child, Je - sus lived on earth as Heav - en's
47
Child. Born be - low for the
51
grace of God to show, He was for - ev - er from the Fa -
54
mf
ther Heav - en's Child. When He was
58
grown, His love was shown on a
61
tree be - neath a dark - ened sun.
64
His love would cost His life on the

68
(opt. div.)
cross, So we can be - come
72
rit.
a tempo
Heav - en's child,
75
unis.
heav - en's child We can live with Him
78
as heav - en's child.
81
Born be - low, but be - cause of grace we'll
84
go to be for - ev - er with the Fa - ther, heav - en's
87
1
2
(opt. div.)
child. child. In
91
heav - en with the Fa - ther, For - ev - er with the Fa -
94
rit.
unis.
ther, heav - en's child!

Nick E Notes "Vowel" Attire

Pronounce the Vowels Correctly

Musical Decoding

Use this code to solve the messages your teacher gives you!

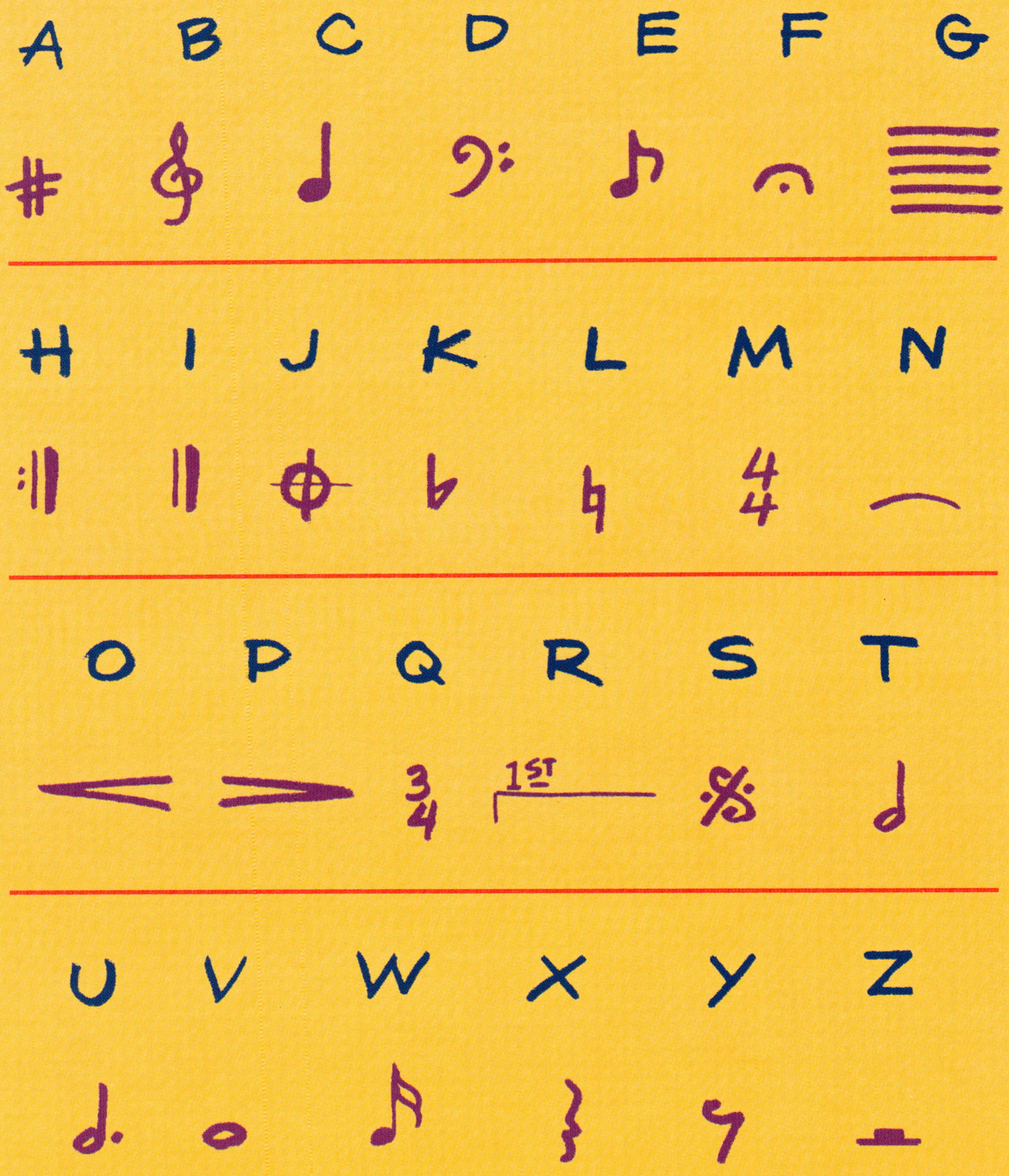

A B C D E F G

H I J K L M N

O P Q R S T

U V W X Y Z

Meet *Isaac Watts*

Stick Wick Saga Melodies

Sing the melodies assigned to you when the teacher holds up your number and help tell the story.

THE MINISTRY OF Twila Paris

A Career in Contemporary Christian Music.

MISSION MINDED MUSICIANS

Meeting the Manuel's / Music Missionaries

A youth choir singing at a Children's Home

A youth choir singing in Olney, England

Children and Their Instruments from Around the World

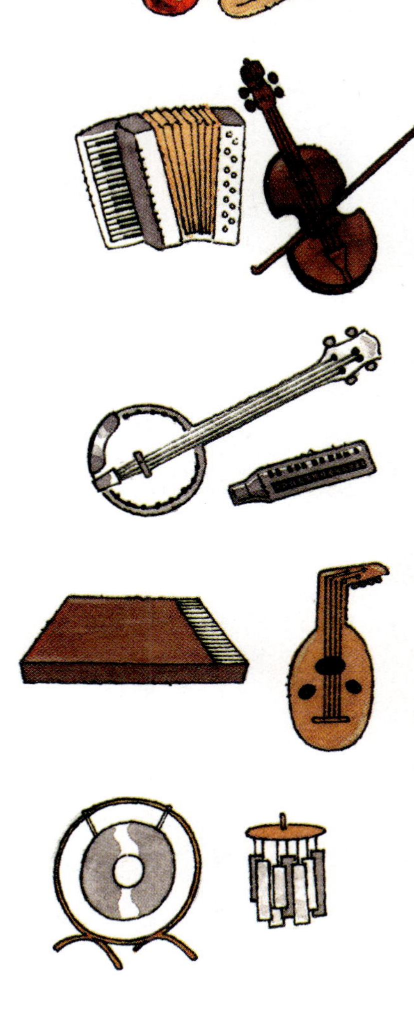

A. Japan

B. Switzerland

C. South America

D. Africa

E. America

F. Pacific Island

G. Russia

FROM FIRST SOPRANO TO BARITONE
HOW MY VOICE CHANGED

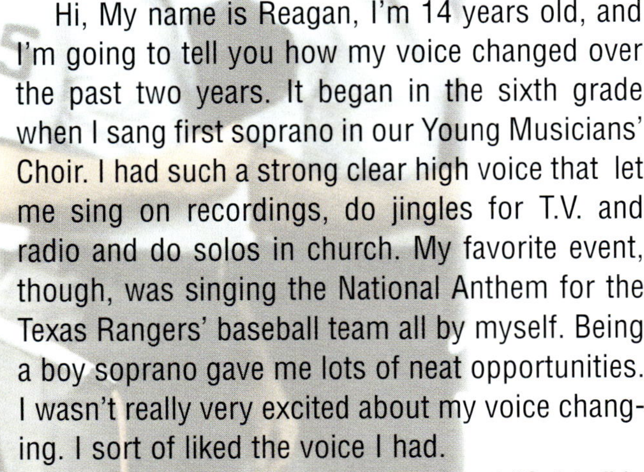

Hi, My name is Reagan, I'm 14 years old, and I'm going to tell you how my voice changed over the past two years. It began in the sixth grade when I sang first soprano in our Young Musicians' Choir. I had such a strong clear high voice that let me sing on recordings, do jingles for T.V. and radio and do solos in church. My favorite event, though, was singing the National Anthem for the Texas Rangers' baseball team all by myself. Being a boy soprano gave me lots of neat opportunities. I wasn't really very excited about my voice changing. I sort of liked the voice I had.

At Christmas I was doing the part of "Gabby" in the "Don't Be Afraid Brigade," and I began to notice my high notes sounding a little huskier than usual. By May I had grown six inches and my speaking voice began to sound more like my dad's instead of my mom's. In April, our choir was singing for the Young Musicians' Choir Festival. I could comfortably sing all the melodies an octave lower than written. Of course, that sounded terrible in a children's choir, so I just sang alto lightly in my head voice and no one knew that our children's choir really had a wobbly baritone in it.

By fall I was singing in the youth choir and reading the bass clef where my voice now belonged. I was the only seventh grade boy whose voice had begun to change, and the only one who had to shave too. My voice really dropped fast although some of my friends voices have changed more gradually. Now I'm working on expanding my upper range again. It took a while for me to feel comfortable with my new singing voice and to adjust to new sounds. Being in children's choirs really helped me. I already knew how to support my tone, sing in a head voice, read music, and sing correct vowels. It made my transition easier. When some new kids come to youth choir, they get lost in the music and sometimes can't even match tones. It makes me grateful I have always gone to choir. Singing is still fun and youth choir is one of my favorite activities. If you're a guy, be patient when your voice changes and keep singing!

Your Friend,
Reagan

My God Is Mighty!

(With energy and excitement)

All:	My God Is Mighty!
Speaker #1:	The Lord is my rock!
Speaker #2:	The Lord is my deliverer!
Speakers #1 & 2:	The Lord is my fortress!
All Boys:	My God is my rock, in whom will I take refuge!
All:	My God Is Mighty!
All Girls:	I love you, O Lord, my strength!
Speaker #3:	He is my shield and the horn of my salvation!
Speaker #4:	I call to the Lord, who is worthy of praise!
Speaker # 3 & 4:	Great is the Lord, and most worthy of praise!
All Boys:	Mightier than the thunder of the great waters!
All Girls:	Mightier than the breakers of the sea!
All:	The Lord on high is mighty! My God is mighty!

(Sing "My God is Mighty")

Text from Psalm 18: 1-3; Psalm 48:1, and Psalm 93:6

Keys to Your Heart

Revelation 3:20

"Here I am! I stand at the door and knock. If anyone hears my voice and opens the door, I will come in..."

There is a special place Jesus wants to be, and that is in our hearts. Want to know how? Each key below has a special clue that can help you know how to open the door to your heart.

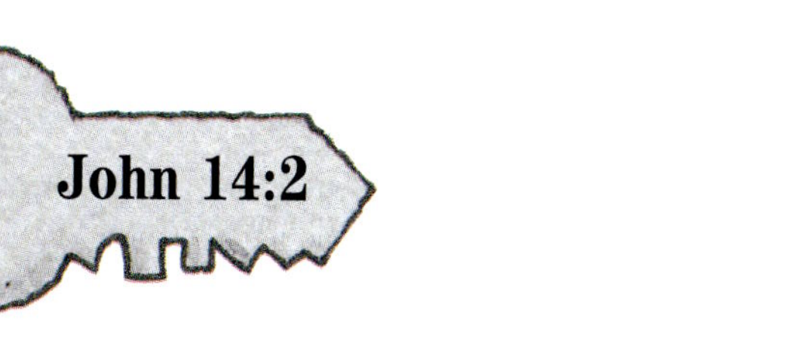

Heaven is a happy place, and Jesus is there now getting it ready for us!

When we disobey our parents, or lie, we are sinning. God tells us that everyone sins, and no one is perfect. God sent Jesus to take the punishment of our sin, and die for us on a cross.

...While we were
yet sinners,
Christ ________
for ______.

The key reminds us that Jesus' blood was shed on a cross that we might be forgiven. Jesus died for every one of our sins, and was buried, and He rose again three days later.

John 1:12

To all who received Him,
to those who believed in His name,
he gave the ______ to
become____________.

This key reminds us that when we believe in Jesus, and ask Him to forgive us of our sins, He will come into our hearts, and take away our sin, and live within us FOREVER!

...________with your mouth,
Jesus is Lord, and__________
in your heart that God raised Him
from the dead you will
be saved.

The last key will open the door to your heart if you really want Jesus in your life! Just pray to Jesus that you believe in Him, and ask Him to forgive your sins, and come into your life to live forever, and He will!

Musical Boo Boo's

God expects us to do our best in everything. That includes how we sing! I Corinthians 10:31 says "whatever you do, do it all for the glory of God." When we sing, sometimes we don't always sing our very best to God, because of bad singing habits. Here are some musical boo boo's that if you don't watch out, will creep in on you. Before you sing next time in class or in church, make sure you fix the boo boo's!

Vowels Along the Way

For accompaniment see Leader's Guide, p. 65.

18
yak - a - yak - a on the phone! _ "Oh," "oo."
20
When I'm out of school, I go ___ to the pool, and it's a
21
groov-in', mov-in' way to stay cool. _ "Oo, ah, ay, ee, oh."
23
GROUP 1
I know how to sing _ my vow'ls, _ and I prac-tice ev-'ry day; _
GROUP 2
I know how to sing _ my vow'ls, _ and I
25
(optional repeat and fade)
I know how to sing _ my vow'ls, _ and I prac-tice ev-'ry day; _
prac-tice ev-'ry day; _ I know how to sing _ my vow'ls, _ and I

Musical Bridge

My God Is Mighty

Words and Music by
DAVID HAMPTON and DENNIS KURTILLA
Arranged by Don Schlosser

10
walk - ing with me; I get my strength from the Lord my God.
Gm Dm7 Gm Cm7 D7(#5)
12
Pow - er and strength are
1
mp
Gm Dm7 Gm Eb2 Bb/D
14
His to share; There is - n't a bur - den
Cm F/A Bb Bb/D Eb2 Bb/D
16
He can't bear. My God is
mf
2
Cm D N.C. Gm Dm7 Gm

19
mf
He is the might-y One; I get my strength from Him,
Gm
Dm7
Gm
Gm
mf
21
And He's walk-ing with me.
He is the might-y One;
Cm7
D7
Gm
Dm7 Gm
Gm
Dm7
Gm
24
I get my strength from Him, And He's walk-ing with me.
Gm
Cm7
D7
Gm
Dm7 Gm
27
mp
Pow - er and strength are His to share; There
Eb2
Bb/D
Cm
F/A
Bb
Bb/D
mp

29
GROUP 1 f
is - n't a bur - den He can't bear.
My God is
Eb2
Bb/D
Cm D
N.C.
f
32
might - y,
and He is walk - ing with me; I get my
GROUP 2
f
He is the Might - y One; I get my strength from Him;
Gm
Dm7 Gm
Gm
Dm7 Gm
34
strength from the Lord my God.
My God is
And He's walk - ing with me.
Cm7
D7(#5)
Gm
Dm7
Gm

36
might - y, __ and He is walk - ing __ with me; I get my
He is __ the Might - y One; I get my strength from Him,
Gm Dm7 Gm Gm Dm7 Gm
38
strength from the Lord my God. __
And He's walk - ing with __ me.
Cm7 D7(#5) Gm Dm7 Gm
FINGER SNAPS
40
CHOIR f
My God is might - y, __ and He is
Am Em7 Am Am
f

42
walk - ing with me; I get my strength from the Lord, my God.
Am
Dm7
E7(♯5)
HAND CLAPS
44
My God is might - y, and He is walk - ing with me; I get my
Am
Am
Em7 Am
Am
Em7 Am
47
strength from the Lord my God.
I get my strength from the
(opt. div.)
Dm7
E7(♯5)
Am
Em7
F
Dm7
50
Lord, my God.
Lord, my God!
E7(♯5)
Am
G
A
Am
Am
Em7 Am

I Sing the Mighty Power of God

Words by
ISAAC WATTS

Traditional English melody
Arranged by Don Marsh

For accompaniment see Leader's Guide, p. 128.

He Is the One

Words by
MILTON LeDOUX

Music by
JOANNE BROWN LeDOUX
Arranged by Randy Smith

11
brings us sal - va - tion and __ new life. He is the One, Je -
wash - es the sin and doubt _ a - way. He is the One, Je -
Bb Eb Eb/F F7sus Bb2 Eb F
14
unis.
sus the Son, for He is the Way and the
sus the Son, and He'll make His home in your
(F) Gm Bb Eb Gm
16
Truth and Life. Yes, He is the Way and the Truth, the Life.
heart to stay. Yes, He'll make His home in your heart to stay.
F7 Bb/F Bb Bb Eb Gm Fsus
19
1
2
1 Cm7 Bb2/D F7sus/Eb F7sus
2 Cm7 Bb2/D F7sus/Eb

22
We sing the mel-o-dies of the Teach-er of love, the
F7sus/Eb F Bb Eb F/Eb Bb2/D Gm
25
Heal - er and the King. Cre - a - tor and Sav - ior and
Cm7 F Bb2 Eb F
28
Lord up a - bove, Je - sus is why we sing!
Bb2/D Csus
30
(opt. div.)
He is the One, Je -
Fsus Gsus C2 F G7sus

33
sus the Son, who's mak - ing a place for you __ and me!
(G7sus) C C F F/G G7sus
36
unis.
He is the One, Je - sus the Son, and we'll praise His name for e -
C2 F G Am C F Am
39
div.
ter - ni - ty. Yes, we'll praise His name for e - ter - ni - ty.
G7 C/G C C F Am G7sus
42
Dm7 C2/E G7sus/F C2(no 3)

Let the Song Go Round the Earth

Words by
SARAH G. STOCK

Music by
BURYL RED
Arranged by Don Schlosser

9
Sound His praise, tell of His worth,
With the sto - ry of His worth,
With the sto - ry now, and
11
Be His name a - dored;
Let the whole earth ring;
Let the whole earth ring;
14
p
Ev - 'ry - where and ev - 'ry - one
Him cre - a - tion all a - dore
p
Him cre - a - tion all a -
p
cresc.

16
mp
Join the grand and glorious song!
Ev - er - more and ev - er - more.
dore.
mp
Ev - er and ev - er -
mp
cresc.
18
mf
Let the song go round the earth,
Let the song go round the earth,
more.
mf
Let the song go round,
mf
cresc.
20
f
Je - sus Christ is Lord!
Je - sus Christ is King!
f
Je - sus Christ is King!
f

22
1
2
Je - sus Christ is
1
2
Je - sus Christ is
1
2
25
King!
Je - sus
King!
Lord Je - sus
28
Christ is King!
Christ is King!

He's My Shepherd

For accompaniment see Leader's Guide, p. 131.

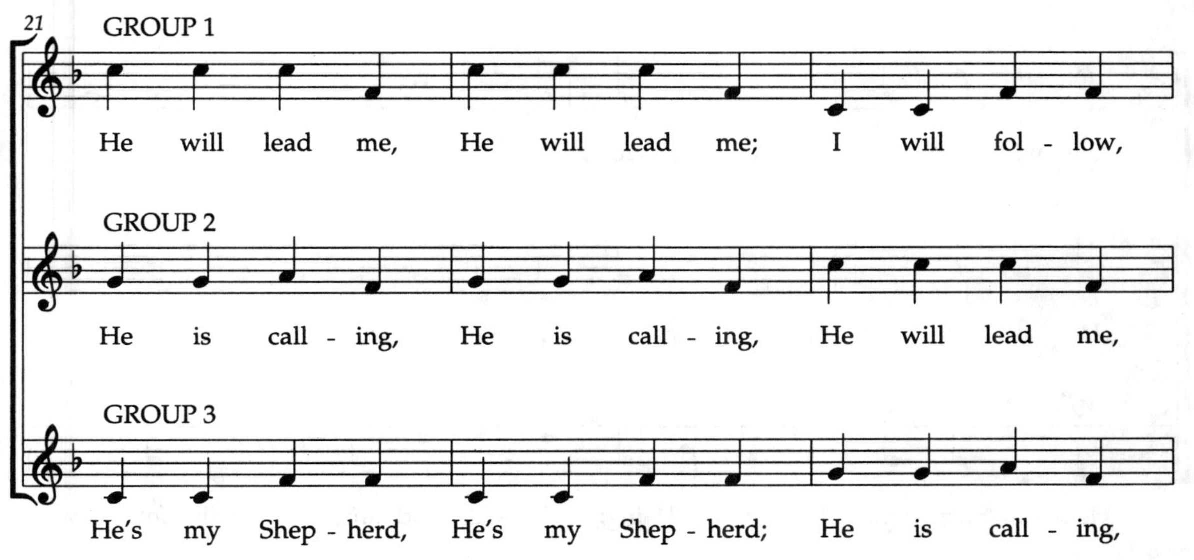
21
GROUP 1
He will lead me, He will lead me; I will fol - low,
GROUP 2
He is call - ing, He is call - ing, He will lead me,
GROUP 3
He's my Shep - herd, He's my Shep - herd; He is call - ing,

24
I will fol - low. I will fol - low, I will fol - low; I will
He will lead me, I will fol - low, I will fol - low; I will
He is call - ing; He will lead me, He will lead me; I will fol - low,

28
rit.
a tempo
mf
fol - low. He's my Shep - herd, He is call - ing;
rit.
a tempo
mf
fol - low. He's my Shep - herd,
rit.
a tempo
I will fol - low.

32
He will lead me, I will fol - low;
I will fol - low,
He is call - ing; He will lead me, I will fol - low.
mf
He's my Shep-herd, He is call - ing; He will lead me, I will fol - low.

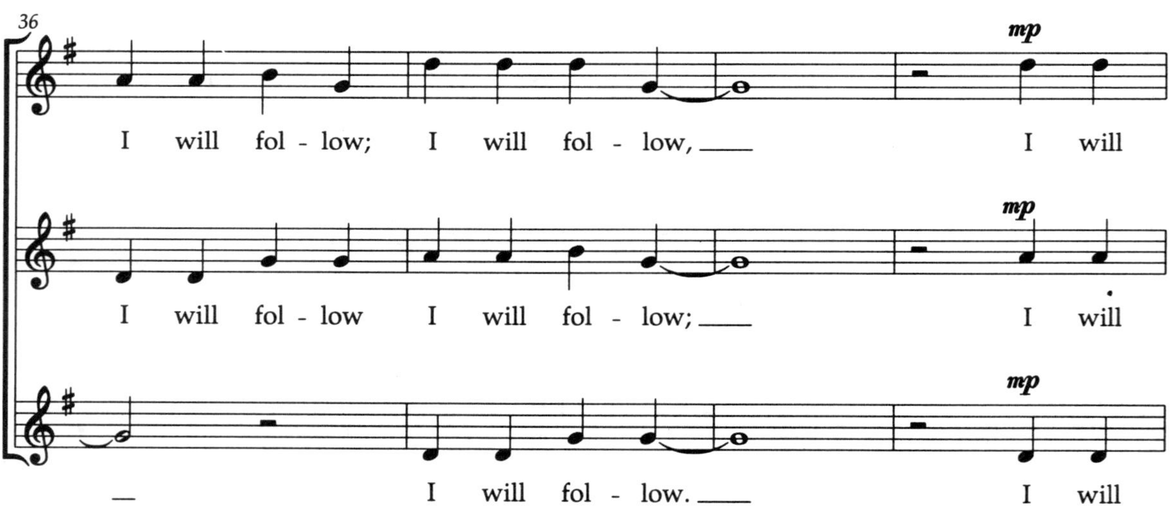
36
I will fol - low; I will fol - low,
mp
I will
I will fol - low I will fol - low;
mp
I will
I will fol - low.
mp
I will

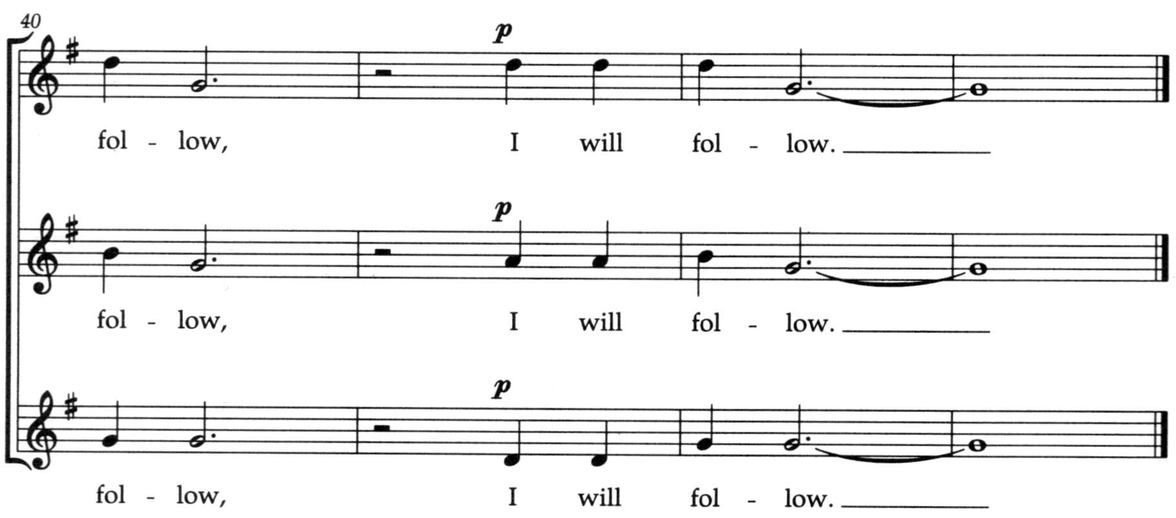
40
fol - low,
p
I will fol - low.
fol - low,
p
I will fol - low.
fol - low,
p
I will fol - low.

Give It All to Him

Words and Music by
KATHIE HILL and CHRIS MARION
Arranged by Barny Robertson

14
what you've got, so give it all to Him. _
Cm7 Bb Cm7 Eb/F F Bb Bb/Ab
First time - SOLO 1
Second time - SOLO 3
17
1. Two mea - sly fish, _ five loaves of bread; _
2. One lit - tle mite, _ one cent or less, _
Eb/G Fsus F Eb F Bb F/Bb Bb Eb F
21
_ was all one boy _ had, Yet a
_ but Je - sus was _ pleased, when He
Bb F/Bb Bb Eb D7 Gm
First time - SOLO 2
Second time - SOLO 4
24
mul - ti - tude _ was fed. _ I don't have much, _
saw one wom - an's gift. _ Rich men a - round _
Csus Bb/C F Gm/F F Eb F

27
I'll give what I can. But my gift is
thought her gift was small. But Je - sus was
B♭ F/B♭ B♭ E♭ F B♭ F/B♭ B♭ E♭ D7
31
great, when I place it in God's hand. What I've
pleased, for she had giv-en her all.
1 CHOIR
Gm Csus B♭ F
34
2
CHOIR f
What I've got, I'll give; what I
F G F C/E
37
give, He takes; what he takes, He makes in - to some-thing great! God
Dm7 G F C/E D G

40
does a lot __ with what you've got, So give it all to Him. _
F C/E Dm7 C Dm7 F/G G
43
1
2
(opt. div.)
_ What I've _ So
1 C C
2 Am Am G/A
47
give it all to Him. So give it all to Him. So
Dm Em F/G G C G/A Am7 Dm Em/D F/G G C G/A Am7
51
give it all to Him! So give it all to Him!
Dm Em/D F/G G C G/A Am7 Dm Em/D F/G G C N.C. C

Stick with It

25
1
CHOIR
nev - er, ev - er stop!
Stick
great you'll feel ___ when you're through!

28
2
GROUP 1
Stick with it, be-cause you nev-er know what
2
GROUP 2
Don't quit; don't stop _

31
God has in store for you. ___ Stick with it be-cause you
do - in' right. _ Don't quit;

34
nev-er know what He'll do with you when _ you're through. ___ He's
don't stop, _ day or ___ night. ______

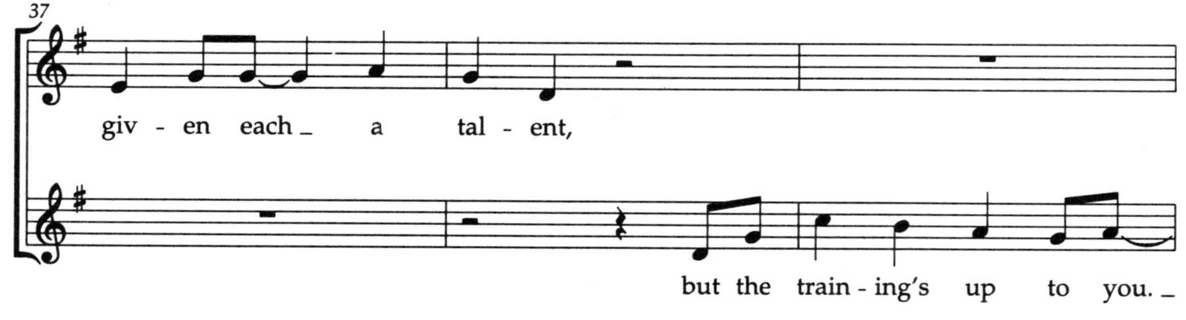
37
giv - en each _ a tal - ent,
but the train - ing's up to you. _

40
So don't ev - er quit, just stick with ___ it.
___ So don't ev - er quit just stick with ___ it.
44
SOLO 1
CHOIR
SOLO 2
Do you think I could draw? Stick with it! But I'll
47
CHOIR
nev - er make As! You can, if you try!
CHOIR: You haven't been listening; ... just stick with it!
49
SOLO 3
3
I wan - na play the pi - an - o.
SOLO: But if I run another lap, I think I'll die!
54
3
GROUP 1
Stick
58
GROUP 1
with it, be-cause you nev-er know what God has in store for you. ___
GROUP 2
Don't quit, don't stop _ do - in' right. _
61
___ Stick with it, be-cause you nev-er know what He'll
___ Don't quit, don't stop _

64
do with you when _ you're through. _
He's giv - en each _ a
day or ___ night. ___
67
tal - ent,
So
But the train - ing's up to you. __
70
don't ev - er quit, just stick with ___ it.
No, don't ev - er quit, just
73
No, don't ev - er quit, just stick with ___
stick with ___ it.
No,
76
it; Just stick with __ it!
don't ev - er quit, just stick with __ it!

Sing and Rejoice

Words and Music by
DAVID HAMPTON and DENNIS KURTILLA
Arranged by Barny Robertson

For accompaniment see Leader's Guide, p. 143.

28
the Lord; With this joy in my heart I'll sing
the Lord; With this joy in my heart I'll sing
31
and give thanks un - to the Lord.
2
and give thanks un - to the Lord.
2
35
I will sing and re-joice, will sing and give thanks un - to
I will sing and re-joice will sing and give thanks un - to
38
the Lord; Won't you sing and re - joice, yes, sing
the Lord; Won't you sing and re - joice, yes, sing
41
and give thanks un - to the Lord? For He
and give thanks un - to the Lord? For He

44
is wor - thy of our wor - ship; And
is wor - thy of our wor - ship; And
47
He is wor - thy of our praise.
He is wor - thy of our praise,
50
I will
our praise.
I will
53
sing and re-joice, will sing and give thanks un - to the Lord;
sing and re-joice, will sing and give thanks un - to the Lord;
56
With this joy in my heart I'll sing and give thanks un - to
With this joy in my heart I'll sing and give thanks un - to

59
_ the Lord. I will sing and re-joice, will
_ the Lord. I will sing and re-joice, will
62
sing and give thanks _ un - to ___ the Lord; Won't you
sing and give thanks _ un - to ___ the Lord; Won't you
65
sing and re - joice, _ yes, sing _ and give thanks _ un - to ___ the Lord?
sing and re - joice, _ yes, sing _ and give thanks _ un - to ___ the Lord?
68
Sing and give thanks, Sing and re - joice,
Sing and give thanks, Sing and re - joice,
72
Sing and give thanks _ un - to ___ the Lord!
Sing and give thanks _ un - to ___ the Lord!

For accompaniment see Leader's Guide, p. 150.

15
King, Je - sus is King, Je - sus is King; Je - sus is

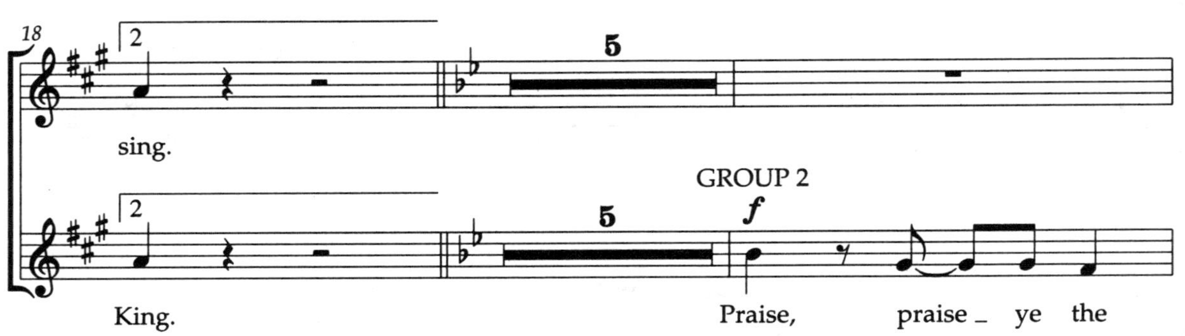
18
2
5
sing.
GROUP 2
f
King.
Praise, praise ye the

25
Lord, Praise ye the Lord, Praise ye the

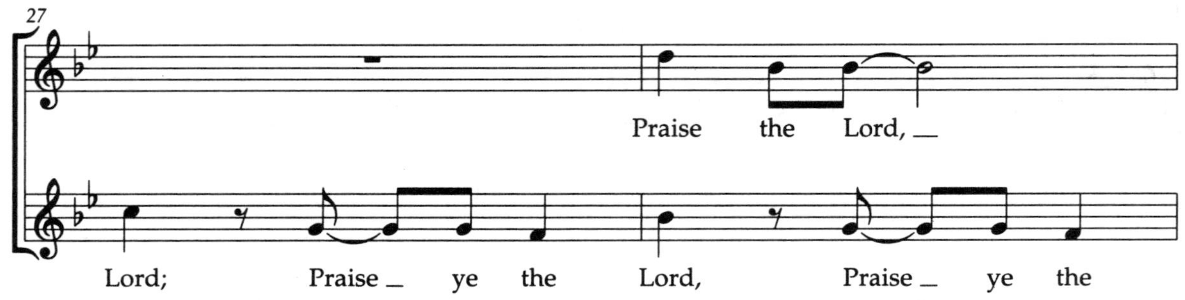
27
Praise the Lord,
Lord; Praise ye the Lord, Praise ye the

29
He's my Sav - ior, so I'll praise the Lord.
Lord; Praise ye the Lord, Praise ye the

31
Add my voice to make a joy - ful chord _
Lord; Praise _ ye the Lord, Praise _ ye the
33
to my King _ of kings.
Lord; Praise _ ye the Lord, Praise _ ye the
35
Lord _ of lords,
Lord; Praise _ ye the Lord, Praise _ ye the
37
Praise _ the Lord,
Lord; Praise _ ye the Lord, Praise _ ye the
39
Praise _ the Lord. Je-sus is Lord!
Lord; Praise _ ye the Lord. Je-sus is Lord!

He Will Be with You

Words and Music by
DAVID HAMPTON and DENNIS KURTILLA
Arranged by Randy Smith

Gently (♩ = 80)

20

C G/B F/A C2/G C/G F

6

First time - CHOIR
Second time - SOLO *p*

1. If I had on - ly one
2. ev - er I feel like I'm

C/E Dm C Gsus G C C/E

11

thing I could say, just one thing be - fore I
lost and a - lone, like no one else knows I am

F C/E F C/E

15

go, I'd tell you that Je - sus is
there, I think of the Sav - ior who's

D/F♯ G C G/B

19
God's on - ly Son, who loves you and wants you to
right by my side, who's al - ways as close as a
F/A C/G F C/E Csus/D C
23
CHOIR (both times)
(opt. div.) mp
know.
prayer.
He will be with you wher -
G/B F2/A G E7/G# Am C/G F
mp
27
ev - er you are; He wants to for - give all your
F/C C G Am D7
31
sin. And when you ask Je - sus to
Gsus G C G/B

35
live in your heart, He'll o - pen the door and come
F/A
C/G
F
G7sus
G7
39
1
SOLO p
in.
2. When -
1 Am
F
G7sus
G
43
2
(opt. div.)
in.
Oh, how He wants to come
2 Am
C/G
F
C/E
Dm7
G7sus
G7
47
in.
C
Cmaj7/B
F/A
Cmaj7/G
F
Gsus
G7
C
C